A Family in Central America

This book takes you on a trip to Costa Rica, in Central America. There you will meet Zacarias and Adelaido Figueroa, Central American Indians living in the remote forest. Zacarias will tell you about the life of a small farmer. You will also discover what the rest of the family do, what their home is like, what they eat and what their interests are.

FAMILIES AROUND THE WORLD

A FAMILY IN
CENTRAL AMERICA

Peter Otto Jacobsen and
Preben Sejer Kristensen

The Bookwright Press
New York · 1986

Families Around the World

A Family in Australia
A Family in Central America
A Family in Colombia
A Family in China
A Family in France
A Family in Greenland
A Family in Hawaii
A Family in Holland
A Family in Hong Kong
A Family in Iceland

A Family in India
A Family in Ireland
A Family in Japan
A Family in Mexico
A Family in the Persian Gulf
A Family in Switzerland
A Family in Thailand
A Family in the U.S.S.R.
A Family in West Africa

First published in the United States in 1986 by
The Bookwright Press
387 Park Avenue South
New York, NY 10016

First published in 1985 by
Wayland (Publishers) Limited
61 Western Road, Hove
East Sussex BN3 1JD, England
© Copyright 1985 Text and photographs
Peter Otto Jacobsen and
Preben Sejer Kristensen
© Copyright 1985 English-language edition
Wayland (Publishers) Limited

ISBN 0–531–18081–6
Library of Congress Catalog Card Number: 85–73585

Phototypeset by Kalligraphics Limited
Redhill, Surrey
Printed in Italy by G. Canale and C.S.p.A., Turin

Contents

Between two continents

As our plane comes in over the Caribbean Sea we catch glimpses far below us of Central America, the narrow strip of land (shaped rather like a dog's hind leg) that links the continents of North America and South America.

It is difficult to believe that long ago this land did not exist, but that is what scientists believe. At one time North and South America were quite separate. Then, about 20 million years ago, the plates of the Earth's crust began to push

Mist rising from the tree-covered hillsides of Costa Rica.

against each other so that the floor of the Pacific Ocean moved toward the floor of the Caribbean.

The force of this movement created volcanoes, which rose from the rocky seabed as a chain of islands. By about 3 or 4 million years ago, this new land had grown and joined together into one mass, forming a bridge between the two continents. This is the area that we now call Central America.

Today the land is divided into seven countries: Guatemala, Belize, El Salvador, Honduras, Nicaragua, Costa Rica and Panama. We are going to visit the Figueroas family. They are a Central American Indian family who live in the remote forests of Costa Rica.

Central America is a strip of land, only 520,000 sq. km. (200,000 sq. mi.) in area, linking the continents of North and South America.

We arrive in Costa Rica

The Indians were the earliest people to live in this part of the world. Thousands of years ago they traveled into Central America from the north. Some of these people, such as the Maya and the Aztecs, went on to create powerful and splendid civilizations in Central America. Then, in 1502, Christopher Columbus sailed his ships across the Caribbean and claimed possession of the new territory he discovered for Spain.

Within a century the land had been taken over by Spain and settled by Spanish colonists. Today, although some Indians and some Indian languages still survive, Spanish is the language spoken by almost everyone in Central America.

Unfortunately the countries of Central America have had a stormy and often unhappy history. Most of them are still in political upheaval. However, Costa Rica, where we are headed, has been the

One of the many impressive volcanoes in Costa Rica.

Above: *Buildings in Guatemala built in the Spanish-style of Architecture.*

Below: *The map shows the countries of Central America.*

CENTRAL AMERICA

MEXICO

CUBA

BELIZE

GUATEMALA

Caribbean Sea

EL SALVADOR

HONDURAS

NICARAGUA

• SAN JOSÉ

COSTA RICA

Buenos Aires •

PANAMA

most settled and successful of them all.

As we fly in over the rain forest that covers so much of this part of the world, we are amazed at the extraordinary beauty of the landscape and the rich greenness of the trees and plants. In places bare rocky volcanoes push into the sky, some still sending up columns of steam and gases from huge craters.

By the time the plane comes in to land at San José, the capital city of Costa Rica, we are really looking forward to having a closer look at the land and its people.

Across the mountains

A street scene in San José, capital of Costa Rica.

After the long flight we are glad to rest for the night in a hotel in the city of San José. But the next morning we are eager to begin the most exciting part of our journey – the ride across country to meet the Figueroa family.

The family lives in a remote area in the south of the country, and we have to take a bus for the first part of the journey. The ride is quite an experience!

As the bus takes us over the mountains of Costa Rica, we look down at thick banks of cloud lying in the valleys below us. The journey continues for hours, up above the clouds, through green and deserted mountains with only an occasional house.

We are surprised to find that the bus stops now and again to pick up passengers. It is difficult to see where they come from, but suddenly they appear by the roadside waiting to be picked up. Most of the men are wearing special Costa Rican versions of the cowboy hat.

Everyone seems happy and contented, with tanned complexions and a sense of humor. When a man asks the driver to stop the bus, no one is in any doubt as to why – he has drunk too much! This causes a great deal of laughter.

At last, after driving for four hours, we are dropped off at a small town called Buenos Aires. Unlike its famous namesake in Argentina, this Buenos Aires has only a bus station, a few cantinas (bars), a school, a church and a collection of houses. This is the Figueroas' nearest town.

A jeep has been provided to take us the rest of the way.

Now there is no road at all, just the occasional track made by other vehicles. The red-colored earth is covered with stones and deep pot-holes. The jeep bounces and bumps across the ground and we have to hold on tight. Fortunately the ground is still quite dry. Our driver tells us that this area is impassable after heavy rain.

The jeep continues across the desolate, wild land until at last we approach a little cluster of houses – our destination.

Above: *These two girls are of Spanish descent.*

Below: *Our jeep bounces its way across the rough track.*

The Figueroa family

The people come out to meet us as we arrive, and they are friendly and hospitable. They are excited to see us, as visitors are rare in this remote place.

Zacarias Elizondo Figueroa comes forward and introduces himself and his family, his wife Adelaido and their six children and one grandchild. These are the people we have traveled so far to meet.

When we have exchanged greetings, Zacarias takes us to see their wooden house, which he built himself. It took him three months to build. The house is

Zacarias Figueroa shows us the inside of the house he built.

Valerio, Zacarias's father-in-law, shows us some of the family's animals.

not very large, having only three rooms and a kitchen, but it is very attractive. The family's cattle, pigs and chickens wander around freely outside.

The children cluster around us excitedly, wanting to hear about our jour-ney. Zacarias and Adelaido have five daughters and one son. Julia, the oldest daughter, is 17 and is married to a local farmer. She has a baby of her own, a son called Danilo, who was born quite recently.

Julia's younger sisters are named Clara, Marta, Maria and Alicio, who is only one year old. José, the son, is 12.

Zacarías

Zacarias is 40 years old. He is a farmer, owning a small piece of land about a quarter of an hour's ride on horseback from the house. There he grows rice, corn, beans and *yuca*. The soil is very poor, however, and farming is difficult. The little plot of land provides not much more than the family needs for its own use. But Zacarias is a free man. He has no rent to pay and he is his own boss.

They grow most of their own food. Coffee and spices are the only things they have to buy. Zacarias explains that if they do not have enough money to buy these things, they either butcher or sell one or more of their cattle.

He tells us that life was different when he was younger.

"In the old days," he begins, "we had

Zacarias rides everywhere on horseback, his only method of transportation.

Above: *Zacarias owns a small piece of land where he grows most of the family's food.*

a tradition of helping each other with the harvest. We didn't receive any money for helping, but the person we helped would give us *chicha* – an alcoholic drink made from corn.

"When we finished work we would settle down to drinking the *chicha*. Then there was a real party! We still do it, but not as much as in the old days."

Zacarias' father-in-law, Valerio, lives next door. He is 61 years old, and thinks life has changed for the better.

"I cannot read or write," the old man explains. "There were no schools when we were young. We had to work for nothing for each other then. We drank a lot of *chicha*. We drank for many days in a row. We didn't get paid for our work. Nowadays it's better. Everyone goes to school, we drink less and we're paid for the work we do."

Below: *Valerio is proud of his great-grandson, Danilo, and enjoys playing with him.*

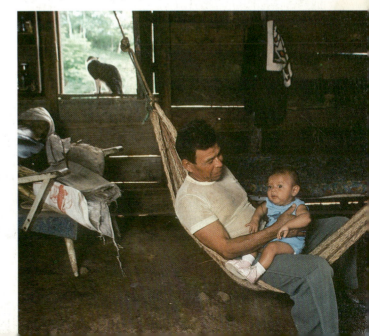

Adelaido

Alicio, the youngest daughter, is not yet old enough to help her mother around the house.

Adelaido also works hard, washing, cooking and doing housework. She is usually up by three or four o'clock in the morning and she works until around five or six in the evening.

When she has time she likes to sew. Her husband and son wear ready-made clothes, but Adelaido makes clothes for her daughters.

Proudly, she points to her old sewing machine beside the bed in the bedroom. "That is my machine," she says. "I use it to make the girls' dresses and skirts."

On the farm it is Zacarias who makes the decisions, but in the house it is Adelaido who is in charge. "The children are expected to help, of course," she says. "Each morning Zacarias and I decide which child shall do what. I want to bring up my daughters so that they can cook and look after a home. They should learn everything about the home.

"One other thing they must learn, too, and that is to respect other people. That's very important."

We ask her if she has any other particular hopes for the future.

"Yes, I hope that there will always be enough food in the house," is Adelaido's firm reply.

Julia, Adelaido's oldest daughter, with her baby son.

A humble life

The Figueroa family live a humble life, with no luxuries, but they do try to go to church every Sunday. It isn't always possible. Sometimes the weather prevents them from going, by making the rough land impassable. However, their Catholic faith is important to them.

Zacarias and Adelaido were married in church.

"We had known each other for many years," explains Zacarias. "I lived farther out in the country than Adelaido, so when I rode into town I had to ride past her house. I was 22 and she was 17 when we were married in the church.

"After the wedding we had a reception for 40 people. There was music and dancing until dawn. Nothing was spared.

When the rains come, this track can be very difficult to ride across.

Above: *The laundry is washed in the river.*
Below right: *Cattle are valuable possessions.*

There was plenty of food and drink."

As a farmer with a poor piece of land, he has to work hard. But he still has some time for hobbies.

"I like to go fishing in the river. The river runs nearby, and we do our washing there. I also like to play soccer."

We ask him how he feels about the future.

"I believe in a good future for myself, my wife and my children. The only time I am worried is when the crops are poor and we cannot get enough to eat."

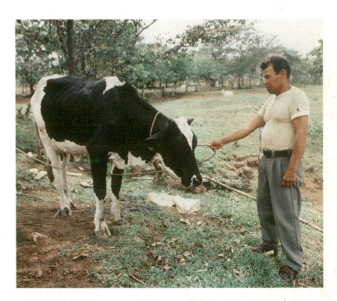

José

José, the son, is 12 years old and goes to school in the nearby town for three hours a day.

"My favorite subject is mathematics," he tells us. "Apart from that I like to play soccer. I don't know what I want to do when I grow up."

We ask him what work he does around the house.

"Well, I chop the wood," he explains, "and I help my father to look after the animals."

José has a best friend, who is in the same class at school.

"He helps me look after the animals," explains José, "and when we have time we like to go fishing together, or we play soccer."

José enjoys mathematics, soccer and fishing.

Although he has never been to the movies, José has once been to a circus. It was, he says, very exciting. He doesn't get an allowance, but once in a while his father gives him some money.

"If you suddenly had a lot of money," we ask, "what would you spend it on?"

José helps his father and grandfather to look after the animals.

José doesn't have to think twice about that.

"I would use it to buy some shoes and clothes," he says.

Five daughters

The Figueroas have five daughters. The oldest, Julia, is seventeen. The youngest is Alicio, who is not yet two years old.

Between them range Clara, Marta and Maria who, like José, attend school for three hours a day. When they come home they help their mother to keep the house clean, but they also like to play by the river when they can. There are no enter-tainments for them, no television or movies, so they have to make their own games. They are intrigued by us and, judging by their giggles, they find us very amusing. But they are shy about talking directly to us.

We remember what their grandfather, Valerio, told us about his lack of educa-tion. These children are getting a better chance. In Costa Rica as a whole, about 92 percent of the children now attend

Clara expects to marry when she is still a teenager, like her sister Julia.

Above: *Maria and Marta go to school for three hours a day and also help in the house.*

Adelaido and Zacarias have five daughters and one son.

elementary school. There are few people left who cannot read or write – about six people out of a hundred. This is fewer than in any other Central American country.

What sort of future does Zacarias expect for his children?

"If they have the ability to read, then they can do that," he says, "but they shouldn't try to do more than their ability allows. I do hope that one of them will take over the farm, though."

Mealtime

Adelaido has been busy in the kitchen. Now she comes in to offer us a meal, and we are happy to accept her invitation. Most of the family's food is grown by Zacarias. Today we are to have the family's favorite dish: rice and beans.

As we sit down to eat, Adelaido tells us how the dish is cooked. There are three parts to the meal: rice, beans and spaghetti. The parts are each cooked separately, and then served together in portions on the same plate. It is a simple meal, but very tasty and filling.

Bananas grow well in this climate and are an important export crop for Costa Rica.

Above: *Adelaido cooks us a delicious dinner of rice and beans.*

Above: *The finished dish.*

25

What is a Central American Indian?

The Figueroas are Central American Indians, whose ancestors lived in this part of the world long before the arrival of the Spanish. For many years Indians have been the poorest and most neglected section of the population. Now this area of Costa Rica has been set up as a fully-Indian district. An official organization looks out for their interests and tries to improve their living conditions.

As we sit and relax after our meal, we ask Zacarias what it means to him to be an Indian.

"Of course the name 'Indian' is wrong," he explains, "but that is what people call us. I am told that our ancestors, like North American Indians, originally came from Asia many thousands of years ago. Many of our people did not survive the arrival of the Europeans. Today there are very few of us left in Costa Rica, only a few thousand here in the south and a few hundred more on the northern plains.

"But I am proud to be an Indian. To me, an Indian is someone who helps his neighbor. If he has something his neigh-bor needs, then he shares it with him. We help each other when we can. Apart from this we have our music, our traditions and our own language, of course. I should like my children to marry Indians. We don't try to set ourselves apart from other people, but we do want to try to preserve our own culture. That is quite hard. Some of our languages are already beginning to die out."

Many people think that Central American Indians are just like the "Red Indians" they see in cowboy movies, so we ask Zacarias what he thinks of such movies.

"Well," he begins, "I have only been to the movies a few times in my life, but I have occasionally seen American cowboy movies on television in town. I don't like them. To my mind, and the minds of all my friends, these films make fun of the Indian. They exaggerate and do not tell the truth about Indians.

"And, you know," Zacarias continues, "we don't smoke peace pipes like the North American Indians in the movies. We smoke a pipe the way other people smoke cigarettes. If I fall out with some-one, or become enemies with my neighbor, then time must heal the wound. After a while we become friends

A Central-American Indian woman weaving brightly-colored cloth.

This plantation produces coffee and bananas – two of Central America's most important crops.

again. And friendship means helping one another, and sharing things. That is something we Indians believe in."

We sit and talk for a while longer, but eventually it is time for us to leave and begin our long journey back to San José. Fortunately the weather has been fine, so the rough track will still be open.

Adelaido and the girls gather at the door to wave to us. There is much shouting and laughter. Zacarias and his son José then walk a little of the way with us, beside the jeep, to put us on the right track.

When it is time for us to say goodbye to them, too, we wave our farewells from the window of the jeep and watch as the two figures recede into the forest. We are sorry to leave the family, who have treated us with such kindness and generosity.

Zacarias can read and write, unlike his father-in-law. His children are getting even better opportunities at school.

Facts about Central America

Guatemala
Size: 108,880 sq. km. (42,042 sq. mi.).
Capital city: Guatemala City.
Population: 7,698,800.

El Salvador
Size: 21,393 sq. km. (8,260 sq. mi.).
Capital city: San Salvador.
Population: 4,586,544.

Honduras
Size: 112,088 sq. km. (43,277 sq. mi.).
Capital city: Tegucigalpa.
Population: 3,511,000.

Nicaragua
Size: 120,254 sq. km. (46,430 sq. mi.).
Capital city: Managua.
Population: 2,823,979.

Costa Rica
Size: 50,700 sq. km. (19,600 sq. mi.).
Capital city: San José.
Population: 2,403,781.

Panama
Size: 77,082 sq. km. (29,762 sq. mi.).
Capital city: Panama City.
Population: 2,043,000.

Belize
Size: 22,965 sq. km. (8,867 sq. mi.).
Capital city: Belmopan.
Population: 152,000.

The whole area of Central America is about 520,000 sq. km. (200,000 sq. mi.). This is smaller than the state of Texas, in the United States.

Language: Spanish is the main language used by almost everyone throughout Central America. Some Indian dialects are still used in a few areas, and English is the official language of Belize.

Religion: Roman Catholicism is the main religion in Central America.

Climate: Temperatures throughout the region range from the tropical to the temperate. Much of the land is covered with tropical rain forest, which remains hot, damp and green all year. In Costa Rica it is warm and damp all year on the lower land along the coasts, with average temperatures of 27°C (81°F). On the cooler central plateau (where most Costa Ricans live) the average temperature is 22°C (72°F).

Agriculture: Main crops are coffee, bananas, cocoa, and sugar cane, with cotton and rice also being grown.

Industry: There is very little industry in these countries. Honduras has some mining for minerals; El Salvador and Nicaragua produce textiles and processed food; Panama has various light industries.

Glossary

Central American Indians The original inhabitants of Central America. It is thought that they are descended from people from Asia who crossed into North America over the narrow Bering Straits.

Chicha An alcoholic drink made from corn.

Continent One of the large blocks of land that cover the Earth.

Plates The large rigid pieces which make up the Earth's outer layer or crust.

Rain forest A dense evergreen forest in a tropical area where there are high temperatures and heavy rains all year, producing a rich growth of plants and trees.

Yuca Spanish for cassava or manioc, a food plant.

Index

Acknowledgments

All the illustrations in this book were supplied by the authors, with the exception of the following:
Camerapix Hutchison 9 (top), 10 Michael Cannon, Zefa 8, 11 (top), 27, 28. The maps on pages 7 and 9 were drawn by Bill Donohoe.

32